# WOULD YOU RATHER

## SCAN FOR MORE PRODUCTS

steal somethingto steal
a bar of gold

O R



a work of art?

Would you
rather...

tattoo your whole body

O R



make a piercing all
over your body?

to be addicted
to cigarettes

to chewing gum?

to sleep naked

to sleep
in granny's shirt?

**eat two large meals a day**

**eat four small meals a day?**

**to call your ex**

**call your enemy?**

eat frozen pizza for a month

eat only McDonald fries for a month?

# Would you

# rather...

to wear a witch's hat

to have a cat's tail?

only use Instagram

only Snapchat for the
rest of your life? **Would you rather...**

to dominate

be dominated

to be famous
without money

to be rich but forgotten
by people?

Would you
rather...

to get only hugs

only kisses from
a loved one?

use only sugar for
a year

only use salt?

**Would you
rather...**

to have an orderly life

to have continuous
adventures?

# Would you rather...

# saturday night under the blanket

# crazy night at the club?

# Would you

# rather...

# have a premium account for life on Netflix

# YouTube?

to own a vintage

modern house?

# Would you

# rather...

not to have eyebrows

not to have eyelashes?

whisper all the time

scream all the time?

# Would you rather...

spend 3 days with
your idol

have
a million followers?

# not be able to use the computer

## not be able to use the telephone?

# be burned

# buried alive?

to have bad hair cut

hair color?

# Would you rather...

smell like eggs when you burp

have a green cloud every time you fart?

hiccups for the rest
of your life

you constantly feel like
you need to sneeze

# Would you rather...

have hair that grows
really fast and long

that has the same hair
length for the rest of your
life?

know when you will die

how you will die?

# Would you

# rather...

## not to have knees

## not to have elbows?

have a constant

stinging

itchy feeling?

# Would you

# rather...

to lie in a chest filled

with snakes

a chest filled

with spiders?

to have spoons
for fingers

an ax for fingers?

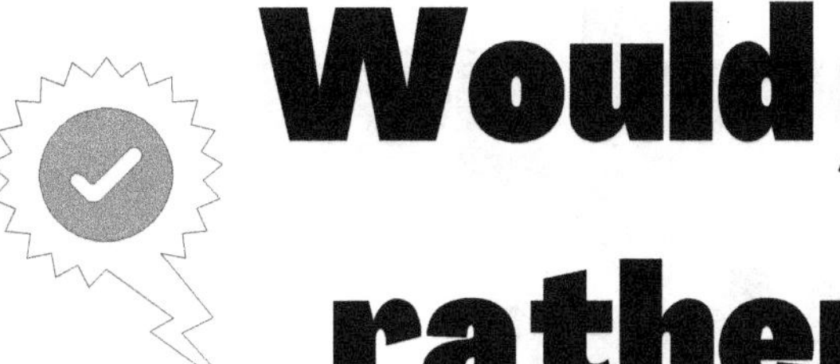

eat your own vomit

eat your own poop?

**not to know your parents**

**to know them knowing that they are serial killers?**

# Would you rather...

**hear squeals in ears**

**see through a fog?**

to live in the Ice Age

in the Middle Ages?

# Would you rather...

to be homeless

to

be in prison for 5 years?

save your family from

the fire and die

save yourself and

let them perish? **Would you**

**rather...**

to have wrinkles

on the face

all gray hair?

smell like garlic
but look nice

smell like flowers but

look disgusting?

**Would you**

**rather...**

stand on red-hot coal

for 20 seconds

hold your hand on
a hot iron for 20 seconds?

have a day that lasts 30 hours
but have more responsibilities

have a day that lasts 20 hours
and fewer responsibilities?

# Would you rather...

to drink a glass of saliva

eat a ball of someone's hair?

to have only 3 hours of sleep
on the most comfortable bed

to sleep on the floor at will?

# Would you rather...

have a fever for a month

be short
of breath for a month?

**dub
an Oscar-winning film**

**appear
in an average film?**

# Would you rather...

**to be resistant to alcohol**

**to be resistant to disease?**

have huge fake breasts

fake vaginas?

# Would you rather...
ride public transport for free

get an old car for free?

to have strength
like a horse

the speed of
an antelope?

# Would you rather...

get a million dollars

have a 70 percent
chance of getting a billion
dollars?

to have red eyes

to see an image
in black and white?

# Would you

# rather...

watch only horror movies
for the rest of your life

watch only fantastic movies?

kill your siblings

kill your loved one?

# Would you rather...

to be a superhero

a villain?

# to have a finger cut off

## a tongue cut off?

# Would you rather...

eat greenie from a friend's nose

## eat his dandruff

not be able to say "I love you"
for the rest of life

not be able to use curses?

# Would you

# rather...

not to have an upper lip

not to have a lower lip?

**to be ridiculed in public**

**to make fun of someone?**

# Would you rather...

**to be spied on by a neighbor**

**catch your parents for sex?**

**eat herring with apples**

**drink a banana and onion cocktail?**

# Would you rather...

**to be an animal shelter owner**

**a retirement home owner?**

to burn with the touch
of your hand

to give someone the chills
every time you look?

# Would you rather...

become a child for one day

change gender for one day?

to have a cold for
the rest of your life

not to hear anything?

# Would you rather...

have 30 small kittens

30 small dogs?

**to lick the pavement**

**chew someone's gum?**

# Would you rather...

**walk backwards**

**walk sideways?**

**wear rubber pants**

**wear acrid wool pants?**

 # Would you rather... 

**have a big red pimple**

**have bad breath all the time?**

**sleep with Voldemort**

**sleep with Dobby?**

# Would you rather...

**shave the monkey's back**

**wash the zombies?**

to be eaten by a snake

bitten by a lion?

Would you rather...

to fight a giant centipede

to fight a giant spider?

to eat slime sauce

to eat fried scabs?

# Would you rather...

have a hangover for a month

be bitten all over your body by mosquitoes?

a sneeze in the face

get a stinky fart in the face?

# Would you rather...

a bath in a bath full
of clipped nails

a bath in a bath full
of sweat and urine?

## to be in a cold, dark room after death

## end up in hell?

# Would you rather...

## to kill a random human

## an animal?

always have dirty underwear

always dirty clothes?

# Would you rather...

have a tapeworm

horrible scars all over your body?

to be alone in the sea
without food

to be alone in the desert
without water?

# Would you rather...

have constant hallucinations

be mentally ill?

not to have friends
for the rest of your life

have 50 false friends?

# Would you rather...

fart at your own wedding

throw up on your wedding
night?

every time you sneeze
have a hemorrhage

pee with foul liquid
when you fart?

eat someone's ear wax

eat a spoonful of your
dirty nails?

have herpes on the lips
all the time

have fingernail mycosis?

# Would you rather...

have a thick hair in
the middle of your nose

pee every time you cough?

that your sweat turns
into sperm

that your saliva turns
into sweat?

# Would you rather...

to lick a toilet seat
in a public toilet

suck blood from
a used tampon?

to be inside when
Toi Toi capsize

smell like garlic
on the first date?

# Would you rather...

speak all your thoughts aloud

not be able to say anything
until the end of life?

**to wipe your friend's ass**

**be rubbed by a stranger?**

# Would you rather...

**suffer from constant abdominal pain**

**have a stuffy nose?**

every time you eat your favorite
food worms come out of your ears

when you drink your favorite
drink spiders come out of your nose?

# Would you rather...

do you have half-filed teeth

teeth entirely with
huge cavities?